Change for Chessie

Tracey's Elementary School

Media Coin Drive

Spring 2004

Life As a
Frog

Victoria Parker

Chicago, Illinois

For information, address the publisher:
Raintree, 100 N. LaSalle, Suite 1200, Chicago, IL 60602

Printed and bound in the United States at Lake Book Manufacturing, Inc.
07 06 05 04 03
10 9 8 7 6 5 4 3 2 1

Library of Congress Cataloging-in-Publication Data:
Parker, Victoria.
   Life as a frog / Victoria Parker.
      p. cm. -- (Life as)
Includes bibliographical references and index.
Summary: Takes a comprehensive look at the life cycle of the frog.
   ISBN 1-4109-0627-2 (Library Binding-hardcover) -- ISBN 1-4109-0653-1 (Paperback)
   1. Frogs--Life cycles--Juvenile literature. [1. Frogs.] I. Title.
II. Series: Parker, Victoria. Life as.
   QL668.E2P298 2004
   597.8--dc21
                          2003008281

Acknowledgments
The publishers would like to thank the following for permission to reproduce photographs: p. 15 Andy Purcell; pp. 4-5 Bruce Coleman (Jane Burton); pp. 22-23 (Feliz Labhardt); p. 6 FLPA (© W Meinderts) Foto Natur; p. 7 Heather Angel; pp. 8, 9 NHPA (© G I Bernard); pp. 10-11, 12, 14 (Stephen Dalton); p. 16-17 Oxford Scientific Films; p. 13 OSF (© Paul Franklin); p. 20-21 OSF (Ian West); p. 18-19 Woodfall Wild Images

Cover photograph reproduced with permission of Naturepl.com/William Osborn

Every effort has been made to contact copyright holders of any material reproduced in this book. Any omissions will be rectified in subsequent printings if notice is given to the publishers.

Some words are shown in bold, **like this.** You can find out what they mean by looking in the glossary on page 24.

Contents

Frog Eggs

Look into a pond. You might see a blob of jelly with black dots.

The blob of jelly is called **spawn.**

The spawn is frog eggs.

Hatching

The eggs **hatch**.

Out come tiny tadpoles.

tail

Tadpoles have long tails. Their tails help them swim to find food.

Growing

In a few weeks, a tadpole begins to grow legs.

The tadpole's legs grow longer.
Its tail gets shorter.

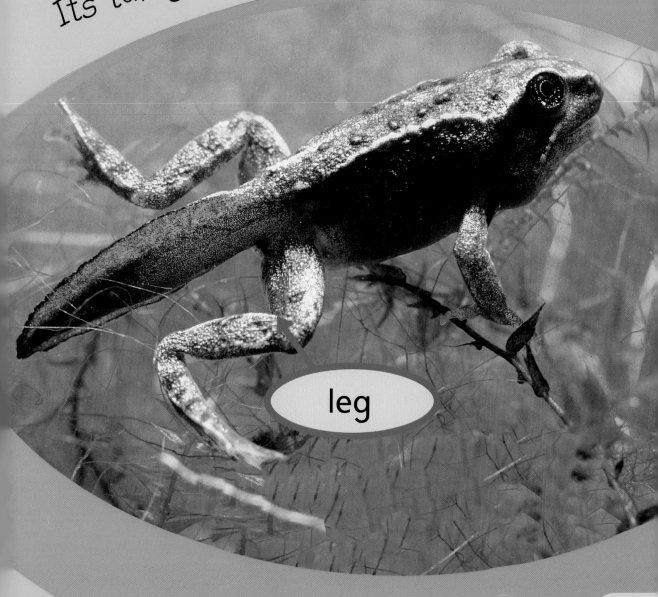

leg

Changing

The tadpole changes into a frog.

The frog has four legs.

A Frog's Life

Frogs live in ponds and rivers.

They spend most of their time in the water.

webbed foot

Frogs use their webbed feet to help them swim.

Life on Land

Frogs spend some time on land.
They hop on their long, strong legs.

Frogs hide in damp, dark places.

Eating

Frogs eat bugs. They catch worms with their sticky tongues.

Mating

Male frogs croak to call a female frog.

The frogs **mate**.

Laying Eggs

The **female** frog lays **spawn** in the pond.

Inside the spawn, new tadpoles are ready to **hatch.**

New Frog Quiz

How did these frogs get into the pond?

Look for the answer on page 24!

Glossary

female girl frog

hatch to come out of an egg

male boy frog

mate when two living things come together to make babies

spawn jelly-like blobs that are frogs' eggs

Frog Life Cycle

Male and **female** frogs **mate.**

Female frogs lay **spawn** in a pond.

Tadpoles grow into frogs.

Tadpoles **hatch** from the spawn.

This is how new frogs got into the pond on pages 22 and 23.

Index